To see more of our books, visit us at:
www.PuppyDogsAndIceCream.com

CLAIM YOUR FREE GIFT!

Visit

PDICBooks.com/Gift

Thank you for purchasing
The Fantastic World of African Animals,
and welcome to the
Puppy Dogs & Ice Cream family.

We're certain you're going to love
the little gift we've prepared for you
at the website above.

Photograph Credits and Copyrights.

FUN FACTS

The greater flamingo is the tallest of all the flamingo species, and the extra height allows them to feed in deeper water. This is beneficial to create less competition for food.

The pinkish coloring of their feathers comes from their primary diet of shrimp which amazingly turns them from gray to their iconic pink color

Flamingos primarily feed with their head in the water because their bill has a filtration system that separates the food from the water

They are often seen standing on one leg, and it is believed that they do this to provide warmth to the leg pulled up against their body and to reduce muscle fatigue

Flamingos can fly, but they must get a running start in order to lift off from the ground and water

Where do they live?
Primarily found along coastal regions of Africa, but also gather at large inland bodies of water

How big are they?
9 lbs = a house cat
5.5 feet tall

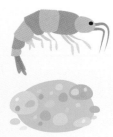

What do they eat?
Shrimp and algae

Greater Flamingo

Phoenicopterus roseus

FUN FACTS

Despite their appearance, warthogs can be very quick and reach speeds up to 30 mph. Female warthogs will form groups with their young and other warthogs, but males prefer to stay isolated until mating season.

The name "warthog" comes from the four wart-like bumps on their face, but these are actually skin-covered tusks

Warthogs love to roll in mud as it cools them off, gets rid of parasites, and acts as both a sunscreen and bug repellent

They have two sets of incisor teeth that form large tusks protruding from their mouth, and though they can be used for protection, they are primarily used to dig up roots for eating

Over time their knees become calloused pads since they kneel down when feeding on grass

Where do they live?
Moist and arid savannas of Eastern and Southern Africa

How big are they?
Male - 210 lbs
4 feet long = a golf driver
Female - 135 lbs, 3.3 feet long

What do they eat?
Short grass and roots

Warthog

Phacochoerus africanus

FUN FACTS

Meerkats are highly social animals that live in groups of up to 40 individuals. They live in extensive underground, burrowed networks that are usually dug out by other ground-dwelling animals.

They have a heightened sense of smell that helps them locate prey hiding underground, and can dig very quickly to uncover them before they escape

Adapted for a life underground, their eyes are protected from dirt and dust by a thin membrane. They can even close their ears

Meerkats will stand on their two hind legs to act as "lookouts" for each other and keep a vigilant eye out for predators, signaling that there's danger with barks and whistles

They have the capacity to memorize the locations of thousands of holes so that they can always run to the closest hole if a predator suddenly appears

Where do they live?
Savannas and rocky landscapes in Southern Africa

How big are they?
1.6 lbs,
1 feet = a classroom ruler

What do they eat?
Invertebrates, insects, small reptiles and rodents

Meerkat

Suricata suricata

FUN FACTS

Nile crocodiles can be very stealthy ambush predators, quietly waiting for unsuspecting prey to take a drink of water before they strike. They go for weeks without feeding, if necessary, for the opportune moment to strike.

The eyes, ears, and nostrils are on the top of their head which allows them to submerge the rest of their body, and be very hard to detect from land

A long, powerful, and flat tail makes crocodiles very strong swimmers and helps them ambush prey on the shores of rivers

Crocodiles have small bumps located all over their body that are part of a sensory system which they use to detect prey through vibrations in the water and even changes in pressure

Their long, powerful jaws produce one of the strongest bites of any animal and, coupled with the shape of their teeth, it is nearly impossible to escape once bitten

Where do they live?
Widely dispersed throughout the waterways of Africa including the Nile River and the Okavango Delta

How big are they?
Male - 1,300 lbs = a golf cart, 18 feet long
Female - 550 lbs, 9 feet long

What do they eat?
Fish, zebra, birds, wildebeest, and antelope

Nile Crocodile

Crocodylus niloticus

FUN FACTS

Gazelles can run around 40 mph, but they are no match to outrun a cheetah. Instead, the gazelle relies on its ability to change direction in the blink of an eye. This throws a cheetah off balance and prevents them from reaching their top speed.

Males have ridged horns that bend slightly backwards, while females have much smaller horns with no ridges or they won't have horns at all

There are multiple species of gazelle, but the Thomson's gazelle is distinguished by the black band on their side, and the patch of white fur that does not extend above the tail

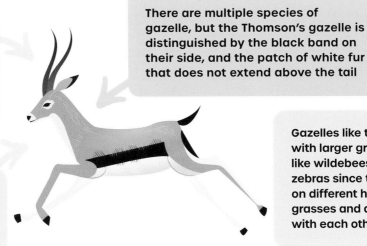

Gazelles like to travel with larger grazers like wildebeest and zebras since they feed on different heights of grasses and don't compete with each other for food

Gazelle's have extremely heightened senses, relying on sight, sound, and smell to detect predators

Where do they live?
Savannas and grasslands specifically in the Serengeti

How big are they?
55 lbs
3 feet long = a guitar

What do they eat?
Short grass

Thomson's Gazelle

Gazella thomsonii

FUN FACTS

African wild dogs are among the most successful hunters in Africa. Their pack hunting tactics, highly communicative social structure, and incredible endurance contribute to their hunts being successful 70-90% of the time.

They have large, round ears which help them locate prey, and also help them keep cool on hot days

African wild dogs are often called "painted wolves" due to the remarkable colored patterns of their coat

Their long legs make them powerful runners, able to maintain speeds of more than 35 mph for several miles at a time

Despite having extra large ears, and a dog's natural good sense of smell, these dogs rely heavily on their sight to track and hunt their prey

Where do they live?
Scattered across savannas, woodlands, and mountainous regions of Africa

How big are they?
40-55 lbs
3 feet long = a golf club

What do they eat?
Warthogs, antelope, zebras, wildebeest, rodents, and birds

African Wild Dog

Lycaon pictus

FUN FACTS

The ostrich is the world's largest and heaviest bird. They also lay the largest eggs, weighing up to 3 lbs. Only dinosaurs have been known to lay larger eggs.

Baby ostriches grow at a rate of 1 foot each month until they are nearly full grown at 6 months old, and at 1 month old they can already run at rapid speeds

They have the largest eyes of all land animals, measuring up to nearly 2 inches wide

With their long powerful legs, an ostrich can run up to 40 mph, can cover over 15 feet in a single bound, and can kill a lion with their kick

Even though the Ostrich cannot fly, they still have wings which they use to help keep balance while running and for mating displays

Where do they live?
Savannas and woodlands throughout Africa

How big are they?
320 lbs = an arcade machine 8 feet tall

What do they eat?
Plants, roots, seeds, insects, lizards, and snakes

Ostrich

Struthio camelus

FUN FACTS

The wildebeest belongs to the antelope family. Their grazing herds make up a large portion of one of the largest gatherings of animals on the planet, amassing over 1 million individuals with other grazing animals like zebras, gazelles, and other antelope species.

They are distinguished from other wildebeests by the black stripes on their neck and a shorter mane of black hair

They have light brown and grayish fur, but seen from afar it can have a silvery-blue sheen which gives them their name

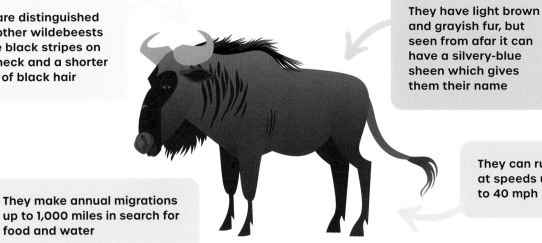

They can run at speeds up to 40 mph

They make annual migrations up to 1,000 miles in search for food and water

Where do they live?

Savannas of Eastern and Southern Africa

How big are they?

500 lbs = a motorcycle
7 feet long

What do they eat?

Tall grass

Blue Wildebeest

Connochaetes taurinus

FUN FACTS

Hippos are often regarded as the most dangerous animal in Africa. They are extremely territorial and can charge at speeds up to 20 mph. The name Hippopotamus has Greek roots which translates to mean "river horse."

The eyes, ears, and nostrils are located on the top of the head so that the hippo can remain almost completely submerged in water

They spend much of their day in water to avoid the heat, and then graze on land at night

A hippo can hold their breath for up to 5 minutes underwater, but they cannot swim or float so they must remain in contact with the bottom to move or stay above the surface

Hippos have very large teeth that can grow up to 20 inches long, and are primarily used for defense and fighting

Where do they live?
Primarily found close to rivers and lakes in sub-Saharan Africa

How big are they?
Male - 5,000 lbs
Female - 3,500 lbs
16.5 feet long = a pickup truck

What do they eat?
Grass and fallen fruit

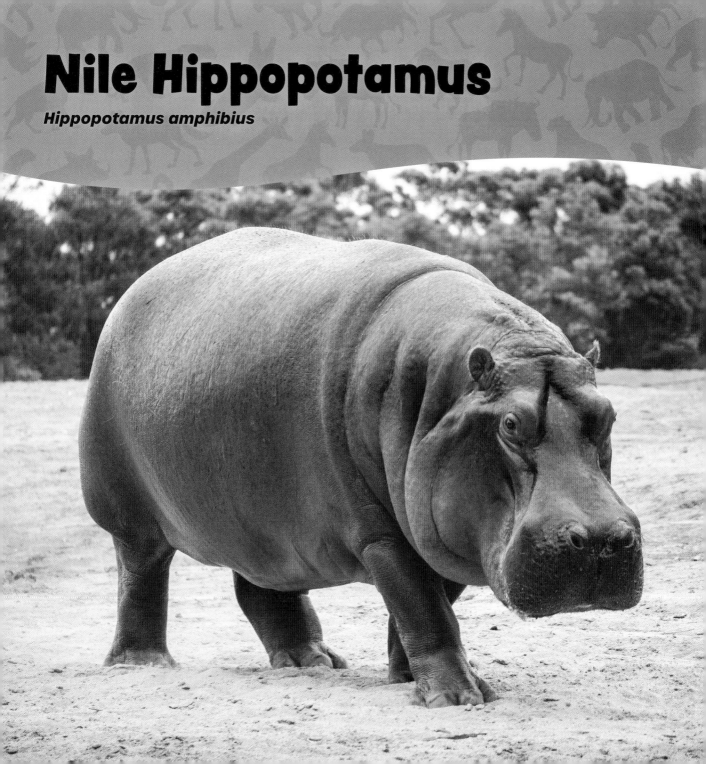

Nile Hippopotamus

Hippopotamus amphibius

FUN FACTS

Leopards are highly skilled climbers, and are often found resting in trees. They will even climb trees with prey in their jaws that can weigh more than them to avoid lions and hyenas from stealing their catch.

They have excellent hearing, and can hear up to 5 times better than humans

The spots on a leopard's coat are actually called rosettes because they resemble the shape of a flower

These powerful cats can reach speeds up to 36 mph, can jump up to 10 feet high, and leap a distance of 20 feet

Their long and strong tails help them balance while climbing trees

Where do they live?
Widespread throughout most of Africa, excluding the Saharan Desert

How big are they?
Male - 130 lbs; Female - 90 lbs
9 feet long with tail =
a ping pong table

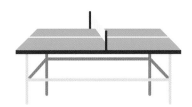

What do they eat?
Impala, gazelle, warthog, hares, and rodents

Leopard

Panthera pardus

FUN FACTS

Hyenas were thought to be purely scavengers, as commonly depicted in cartoons, but they are actually very successful and tactical social hunters.

Their round ears distinguish spotted hyenas from other hyena species

They live in female-led groups called "clans," and they can grow to include 100 individuals

When hyenas eat, they can consume almost the entire carcass, even being able to digest bone without issue

They make many different sounds to communicate a range of signals, including a giggle, which gives them the nickname "laughing hyenas"

Where do they live?
Found widely in grasslands, savannas, woodlands, mountains, sub-deserts, and forest edges

How big are they?
Male - 130 lbs
Female - 150 lbs
4.7 feet long = a tandem bicycle

What do they eat?
Wildebeest, antelope, and scavenged meat

Spotted Hyena

Crocuta crocuta

FUN FACTS

The white rhino is the third largest land mammal, only the Asian and African elephants are bigger. There are five species of rhino, and the southern white rhino is the largest in Africa.

The massive head of a rhino can weigh up to 1,000 lbs alone

They have thick hides that give the appearance of heavy plated armor

The front horn can grow up to 4.5 feet long

The southern white rhino has a characteristically wide and square mouth compared to the smaller and more triangular mouth of the black rhino

Where do they live?
Primarily found in southern Africa

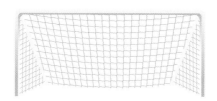

How big are they?
Male - 6,000 lbs,
12.5 feet long = a soccer goal
Female - 3,500 lbs, 11.5 feet long

What do they eat?
Varieties of grass

Southern White Rhinoceros

Ceratotherium simum

FUN FACTS

The giraffe is the tallest land animal on earth. Their height gives them an advantage in reaching food that other herbivores cannot, providing an exclusive food source for the giraffe.

The bumps on their head, often mistaken for horns, are called ossicones and are formed by cartilage

On average, their necks and their legs are each about 6 feet long

Giraffes have a strong, 17-inch long, purple tongue that they use for stripping the leaves off of branches

Giraffes can run up to 35 mph

Where do they live?
Primarily in environments with trees which can include deserts, woodlands, and savannas

How big are they?
Male - 3,500 lbs
18 feet tall = a flag pole
Female - 2,000 lbs, 16 feet tall

What do they eat?
Leafed foliage

Masai Giraffe

Giraffa camelopardalis tippelskirchi

FUN FACTS

Elephants can live to be about 70 years old and are the world's largest land animal. It can take males up to 40 years to reach their full size.

An elephant's trunk has around 75,000 muscles, is one of the most sensitive appendages of any animal, and is used to breathe, drink water, pick up items, and interact with other elephants

African elephants have much larger ears than their relatives in Asia

Elephants take mud baths, and throw dust on themselves to act as a sunscreen

Elephant tusks are enlarged teeth and can aid in ripping bark from trees, digging up roots, or defending against predators

Where do they live?

Savannas and forests of sub-Saharan Africa

How big are they?

Male - 12,000 lbs
Female - 7,500 lbs
21 feet long = a small sailboat

What do they eat?

Roots, grass, fruit, and bark

African Elephant

Loxodonta africana

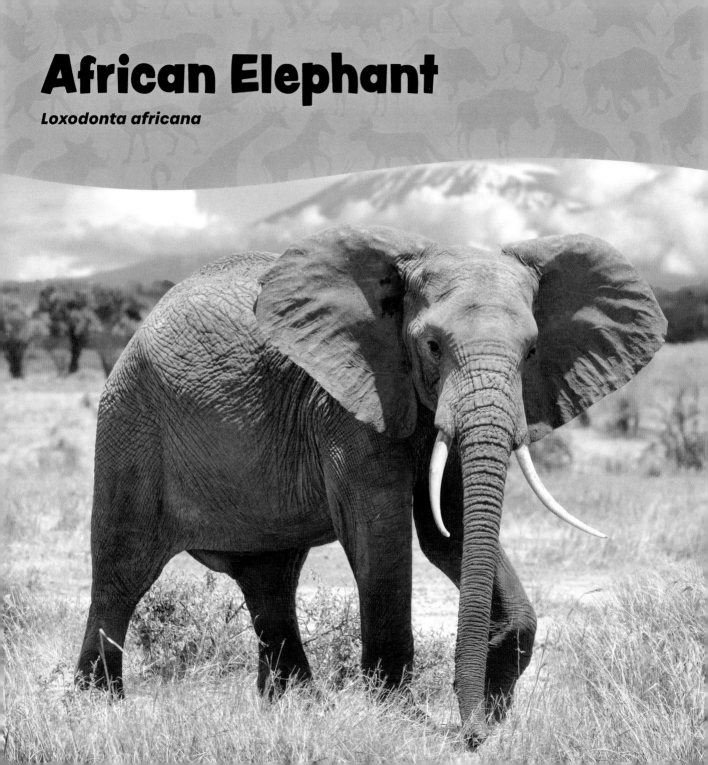

FUN FACTS

The reasoning for their striped pattern is not entirely known, but theories exist that it is to confuse charging predators, or that it helps deter flies. Despite every zebra having these stripes, no two zebras share the same pattern.

The black and white stripes of the zebra make it one of the most recognizable animals in the world

Zebras have good hearing and vision, and often act as an early alarm system for other grazing animals

The variety in their diet gives them a larger range to graze which helps them survive in more habitats

Zebra herds are constantly on the move in search of food, and can travel nearly 2,000 miles each year

Where do they live?
Savannas and open grasslands of Eastern and Southern Africa

How big are they?
550 lbs
7.5 feet long = a pool table

What do they eat?
Grass, leaves, and young trees

Plains Zebra

Equus quagga

FUN FACTS

African buffalo are extremely social animals and can gather in massive herds of 1,000 or more. Traveling in such large numbers is a defensive strategy to reduce the possibility of an attack by lions on an individual.

Males and females both have massive horns that are helpful in fighting off predators, or establishing space in crowded herds

They have very short hair compared to American Bison which is very useful in the much hotter African climate

Buffalo herds primarily feed on grass, and so they are constantly on the move as they graze

African buffalo have poor eyesight and hearing, and rely mostly on their sense of smell

Where do they live?
Savannas, sub-Saharan Africa, and lowland rain-forests

How big are they?
Male - 1,500 lbs
Female - 1,000 lbs
8 feet long = a golf cart

What do they eat?
Grass

African Buffalo

Syncerus caffer

FUN FACTS

Cheetahs are the fastest land mammal, reaching speeds of up to 70 mph, and at top speed they can cover about 21 feet in a single stride.

Cheetahs are light brown/tan in color to blend in with the tall grass, and have solid black spots all over their body

The tail is long and flat, and very important to help them keep balance while changing direction during high-speed pursuits

The dark lines on their face running from their eyes help reflect the sun's glare during the day, and it's a look adopted by athletes to help them with the sun and stadium lights during their games

Cheetah claws do not fully retract which helps give them traction while running after prey

Where do they live?
Primarily found in grasslands of Eastern and Southern Africa

How big are they?
80 - 145 lbs
7.5 feet long with tail = a pool table

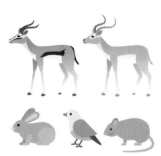

What do they eat?
Gazelle, impala, hares, birds, and rodents

Cheetah

Acinonyx jubatus

FUN FACTS

A group of lions is called a pride. Females are the primary hunters of a pride, and although males hunt too, their main job is to defend their territory against rival males.

Lions can hunt at night because their eyes are adapted to see in low light better than their prey

Male lions have a large mane of hair around their heads that darkens in color with age, and is a sign of dominance

A lion's mighty roar can travel up to 5 miles

Lions can eat as much as 11-15 lbs of meat a day

Where do they live?
Savannas and grasslands in Central, Eastern, and Southern Africa

How big are they?
Male - 420 lbs
7 feet long = 3-person sofa
Female - 280 lbs, 5-6 feet long

What do they eat?
Wildebeest, African buffalo, zebra, and varied antelope species

Lion

Panthera leo

a conservation pioneer worldwide. The organization has worked for 60 years to develop strong, African conservation leadership that focuses on conserving the extraordinary wildlife and wild places. It works with communities who live with wildlife in their "backyards" to create safari businesses that produce benefits that are good for both wildlife and people.

The goal of this book is to introduce young people to a number of animals that are typically seen "on safari." I hope it helps to educate you about the **wonders of our natural world**, and creates a deep appreciation for Africa, whose wildlife is unique, diverse, and unparalleled. Mostly, I hope this book inspires its readers to protect not just Africa's wildlife, but wildlife everywhere, and ensures a bright future for all of Earth's creatures through understanding, support, and conservation.

Craig Sholley
Senior VP of the African Wildlife Foundation

About the Author

Growing up as a kid in central Pennsylvania, I roamed the woods in search of animals, and I dreamed of going to Africa to see the magnificent wildlife. My dream became a reality when I joined the **US Peace Corps**, and I headed off to the Democratic Republic of Congo to teach science for two years in the country's secondary school system. During that time, Peace Corps friends and I planned our first safari, and we spent 60 days camping under stunning night skies in many of East Africa's national parks. My life was changed forever as I vowed to make Africa a big part of my life.

The next time I was back in Africa, I accomplished an even bigger dream by working with acclaimed **gorilla researcher, Dian Fossey**. I had the opportunity to roam the forests of the Virunga Mountains, studying Central Africa's internationally-known mountain gorillas. This work later led to a job directing **Rwanda's Mountain Gorilla Project** – a cutting edge conservation program led by the **African Wildlife Foundation** (AWF). **AWF is Africa's oldest conservation organization**, and it continues to be

LEARN

FUN FACTS

SIZE

WEIGHT

LOCATION

AGES 3-10

THE FANTASTIC WORLD OF
African Animals

Craig Sholley of the
African Wildlife Foundation

FUN FACTS
About Our
Wild Friends